Managing
Stress

Pocket Mentor Series

The *Pocket Mentor* Series offers immediate solutions to common challenges managers face on the job every day. Each book in the series is packed with handy tools, self-tests, and real-life examples to help you identify your strengths and weaknesses and hone critical skills. Whether you're at your desk, in a meeting, or on the road, these portable guides enable you to tackle the daily demands of your work with greater speed, savvy, and effectiveness.

Books in the series:

Leading Teams
Running Meetings
Managing Time
Managing Projects
Coaching People
Giving Feedback
Leading People
Negotiating Outcomes
Writing for Business
Giving Presentations
Understanding Finance
Dismissing an Employee
Creating a Business Plan
Managing Stress

Managing Stress

Expert Solutions to Everyday Challenges

Harvard Business School Publishing

Boston, Massachusetts

Library of Congress Cataloging-in-Publication Data

Managing stress : expert solutions to everyday challenges.
    p. cm. — (Pocket mentor series)
  Includes bibliographical references.
  ISBN: 978-1-4221-1875-7
    1. Job stress. 2. Work—Psychological aspects. 3. Stress management.
4. Self-management (Psychology) I. Harvard Business School Publishing
Corporation.
  HF5548.85.M363 2007
  158.7'2—dc22

                                        2007028830

Contents

Practicing Good Stress Habits   63

Tips for making stress management part of your routine.

Tips and Tools   69

Tools for Managing Stress   71

Worksheets to help you assess life changes that may be adding to your stress, gauge your propensity for worrying, and take stock of the stressors in your workplace.

Test Yourself   75

A helpful review of concepts presented in this guide. Take it before and after you've read the guide, to see how much you've learned.

Frequently Asked Questions   81

Answers to common queries regarding stress management.

To Learn More   85

Further titles of articles and books if you want to go more deeply into the topic.

Sources for Managing Stress   89

Notes   91

For you to use as ideas come to mind.

Mentor's Message:
Why Manage Stress?

It's 7:30 on Friday night, and you're still at your desk—after a long, stressful week in the office. Earlier this week, one of your best employees gave notice. Rumors of a layoff have started circulating around the company. And two hours ago, your boss piled one too many new projects on your plate. You're definitely feeling the adrenaline coursing through your system. But when you stop to think about it, you realize that stress hasn't been limited to just this past week. Things have been tough at work for months now, and it's starting to wear on your nerves.

"Come on," you tell yourself. "Life is always going to be filled with stressful situations. Just ignore it; it'll go away." You're right that life will always present stress. However, a word of caution about trying to ignore it. If you let your stress level soar too high—and stay that way for too long—you, your team, and your company could pay a high price. Sustained, toxic stress can hurt your health and your performance on the job, preventing you from managing your team effectively, which in turn makes it difficult for the team to function at an optimal level.

Yet not all stress is bad. At a reasonable level, it can help infuse you with the energy and drive you need to tackle challenges in the workplace and accomplish important goals. The key to managing stress? Recognize the differences between productive and toxic stress, then assess your stress level. If it's reaching dangerous heights, take charge of your stress through the easy-to-use methods described in this guide. As you'll discover, reducing feelings of vulnerability and powerlessness—the two main ingredients behind stress—is a major first step.

You can't—nor should you—eliminate stress completely from your life. But you *can* learn to manage is so that it works for you instead of against you.

Dr. Edward Hallowell, Mentor

Dr. Edward Hallowell has been an instructor at Harvard Medical School and the founder of the Hallowell Center for Cognitive and Emotional Health in Sudbury and Andover, MA. Dr. Hallowell is a recognized expert on the topics of worry and stress, its causes and cures. He frequently appears in the national news media and on shows such as *Oprah*, *20/20*, *The Today Show*, and *Good Morning America*. He is the author of several best-selling books, including his recent releases, *Dare to Forgive*, *Connect: 12 Vital Ties That Open Your Heart, Lengthen Your Life and Deepen Your Soul*, and *Worry: Hope and Help for a Common Problem*. You can find out more about Dr. Hallowell and his work at his Web site: www.drhallowell.com.

Managing Stress: The Basics

Overload
and Toxic Worry

The word on worry

Are worry and stress really such bad things? Or are we just making a big deal out of a normal state of mind and feeling? Some worry or stress is a necessary and important part of our lives, but in today's fast-paced work world, these natural human responses often spiral out of control and become toxic to our productivity, our peace of mind, and our health. Just see what some experts have to say:

"According to a University of Chicago survey, more than 40% of Americans suffer stress in the workplace."

—NPR, *Morning Edition*

"Job stress today accounts for more than 50% of the 550 million workdays lost annually because of absenteeism."

—K. R. S. Edstrom

"Information anxiety is a chronic malaise, a pervasive fear that we're about to be overwhelmed by the very material we need to master in order to function in this world."

—Richard Saul Wurman

"Job stress [is] a world-wide epidemic."

—World Health Organization

Why be concerned about stress?

So, why be concerned about stress, particularly in the workplace? There are many reasons. What seems normal and familiar—a feeling of worry and anxiety about your daily activities—may be preventing you or your team members from reaching personal and professional goals. Left unchecked, toxic stress can:

- **Reduce productivity.** Toxic stress contributes to decreased productivity, absenteeism, and employee turnover. When employees start making mistakes or slowing down on the job, stay home to avoid stressful work situations, or even quit, hoping to find a less stressful position somewhere else, the productivity of your team or the people you supervise can be directly affected.

- **Affect health.** Too much prolonged stress can make you physically ill and can even kill you. Your body reacts to stress as it would to any dangerous physical situation, raising blood pressure and alerting the senses. This response protects you and can be beneficial for a brief time; however, prolonged stress, worry, and anxiety can strain your body beyond its limits.

- **Drain energy.** Excess worry, stress, and anxiety can drain you of energy, causing your work and your personal life to suffer. You need energy to concentrate well, respond effectively, and judge situations appropriately. Worry uses up your energy, depriving you of the physical, mental, or emotional resources needed to do the job well.

- **Damage relationships.** Stress can disrupt relationships—whether at work or at home. While mismatched personalities in work situations can cause interpersonal conflicts,

What WOULD You Do?

What—Me Worry?

WHEN DANIEL ACCEPTED the promotion, he felt confident that he would be able to handle the increased responsibilities that came with the new position. One month into the job, however, Daniel wondered if he had made the wrong decision. Managing ten direct reports was a full-time job in itself. In addition, he was responsible for generating a new marketing plan, overseeing a huge budget, and serving on multiple task forces. Even though Daniel was staying on top of things, he felt increasingly overwhelmed and tired. He hadn't eaten a proper meal in days. Leaving the office at 8:00 p.m. had become the norm. He wished there was something he could do to make things better, but what?

stress can accentuate these negative feelings or aggravate existing situations, causing small problems to seem large and disturbing the functioning of an entire team.

"More heart attacks occur on Mondays between 6:00 a.m. and noon than during any other time."

—Dr. Harry Dassah

The basic equation of worry

What causes toxic worry? When you feel vulnerable to the perceived threats in your world *and* you feel that you have less power to control your world, your level of worry and anxiety will often increase. In mathematical terms:

Increased vulnerability + decreased power = increased worry

A sense of *increased vulnerability* causes you to exaggerate danger, so that a small problem becomes a huge nightmare. For example, if one month your department's direct costs exceed its budget, you might imagine that the entire year's budget will be engulfed by unforeseen costs. A feeling of *decreased power* causes you to underestimate or forget the power you have to combat danger. For instance, when confronted with the cost overrun, you might forget that you have the power to assess the causes of the overrun and make adjustments to remedy the situation in the following months. *Increased worry* hinders you from making rational decisions and taking positive actions to resolve problems.

This basic equation of worry expresses how toxic worry can arise not from actual danger but from imagined peril. It helps explain how a worried mind can be very creative in anticipating threatening situations that are unlikely to occur.

Bad things really do happen

It is true, however, that bad things really do happen, and at times what seems to be excessive worry is actually appropriate for the situation. To illustrate, if your company is unexpectedly acquired by another, fears of downsizing may be perfectly justified. Or if you're an entrepreneur facing a cash-flow squeeze, and you know the bank could suddenly call in your line of credit, you may feel justified in fearing such an event.

In these situations, the "work of worry," or good worry, can give you the energy you need to deal with the problems. By anticipating the reality, you can prepare possible solutions. The important thing is to know the difference between healthy, protective worry that can help you—and toxic worry that can harm you.

What You COULD Do.

Remember Daniel's worries about
the pressures of his new job?

Here's what the mentor suggests:

Daniel could follow a rational, step-by-step process to examine and improve his stress level. The Evaluate-Plan-Remediate approach works by breaking down the problems that are causing stress into smaller, more manageable units that can be resolved. First, Daniel should identify the problem at hand—namely, that he's overworked and has too many responsibilities. Next, he should think about structuring his time differently. He should set reasonable goals, prioritize them, and break them down into manageable tasks. After that, he should take direct action. He should meet with his supervisor and discuss ways to relieve his workload or delegate some of his responsibilities. By confronting and taking charge of his situation, Daniel will likely reduce his stress level.

Positive Stress and Productive Worry

The dynamic power of worry

Because bad things do happen and because there are high-tension times when we have to be alert, we do need some worry to survive. Worry is our natural defense to a threatening situation, helping us to react quickly and effectively. So up to a point, worry and anxiety are healthy responses.

At first, as anxiety or worry increases, performance also increases. But at a certain point, anxiety becomes excessive and begins to depress performance. An important goal of every businessperson is to find that level of anxiety that will bring about peak performance while avoiding the additional anxiety that becomes toxic to your team or direct reports, as well as to your professional and personal health.

The business value of wise worry

When worry moves from personal fear to clear-headed anticipation, worry energy can make you productive and creative, helping you to discover new solutions to business challenges. Some high-tension worry at work can give you the impetus and adrenaline needed to focus more clearly and perform at a higher level. For example, healthy, positive stress can energize you for action when you have to:

- Meet critical deadlines

- Present an exciting proposal

- Solve new problems

- Feel in control

- Contribute to a team effort

- Learn new skills

- Start a new job

- Deal with a crisis

"Good worry is informed anticipation."
   —Edward M. Hallowell, MD

Wise worry in anticipation can help you prepare for these events, and positive stress during an event can give you the power and vigor to get the job done.

Different strokes for different folks

Some people actually thrive in the high-risk world of trading in the futures market or investing in high-tech start-ups or meeting creative goals in advertising. But other folks prefer a more stable work environment, something more predictable and manageable. The downside of stress is that too much can lead to early burnout and too little can make it easy for people to underproduce. But for each person there is a level of stress that helps that person maximize his or her work goals.

Assessing Your
Stress Level

Do you have a problem?

Wise worry helps many businesspeople perform effectively by giving them the foresight and insight to solve business problems. But toxic worry can distort their perceptions of problems and hamper their efforts to deal with them.

How, then, can you tell whether the stress you feel is healthy or not? How can you discover if you are a problem worrier at work? Simply put, when worry or stress interferes with your productive work, then you do have a problem. Problem worriers exaggerate fears, spend too much time on nonconstructive concerns, fail to make decisions, and are slow to produce results.

If you suspect, or already know, that stress is a problem for you, your team, or your direct reports, start to assess the severity of the problem by looking at both the work environment and individual responses to that environment.

Major work stressors

The common causes of stress in the workplace are (1) *changes in the workplace*—precipitating events that set off a cycle of negative stress; (2) *an unhealthy work environment*—ongoing, underlying, and systemic problems in the office; or (3) *individual responses*—anxious reactions to normal or abnormal situations in the workplace. Typically, the negative stress and toxic worry a person experiences can be related to more than one stressor. Let's take a closer look at each of these causes of workplace stress.

Stressful changes in the workplace include:

- **Change in workload.** If a company reduces the size of its workforce but not its production levels, employees may be asked to take on additional tasks and increase productivity to make up for the loss of personnel. Or employees may be asked to shoulder additional responsibilities on top of their regular tasks during a period of company expansion. In either case, the extra work may cause both resentment and anxiety.

- **Change in pay.** If an employee receives a reduction in pay (perhaps through a reduction in benefits), this would very likely cause worry about budgeting. But even an increase in pay can cause concern if it puts workers into an increased tax bracket or if they feel that they must perform at a higher level to "earn" the increase.

- **Change of job, assignment, or team.** A new job situation is always a stressful time. Not only does a worker have to learn new skills and processes, but new office or team relationships have to be developed as well. All this takes extra energy and attention that can become toxic stress, preventing workers from doing their best.

- **Change in job security.** In this age of high-tech revolution, large corporation downsizing (which often hits middle management the hardest), expected rapid turnover, and rapidly growing global markets, the threat of losing one's job seems to be more constant.

Work environments can feel particularly stressful if employees must contend with:

- **Work overload.** When companies downsize or have trouble finding skilled workers, supervisors often expect their current employees to pitch in and make up the difference in time and labor. Work overload is often the result, adding stress and strain to an already overextended team.

- **Workaholic office culture.** At some high-pressure organizations, the culture demands that employees work long hours and weekends, whether or not the need is real. This culture is marked by intense competition and exhausted workers.

- **Difficult supervisors.** There are managers whose leadership styles simply don't match the professional needs of their direct reports. Some supervisors, for example, believe that pushing their team will increase productivity when the opposite is often the reality—creating a general sense of fear and worry that undermines productivity. Conflict with a difficult supervisor is a major cause of corporate turnover.

- **Negative coworkers.** If an office is filled with an atmosphere of distrust and dissension, the level of stress rises for everyone involved. The causes may be varied—a personality clash, disproportionate workloads, inappropriate or discourteous behavior—but the negative effect is the same.

Some workplaces can foster anxiety and other negative individual responses. For example:

- **Fear of failure.** If a work environment is one of competition and criticism rather than team building and reinforcement, negative thinking can result, turning external critical messages into internal self-doubt and an increased fear of failure.

- **Low self-esteem.** Closely related to fear of failure, low self-esteem occurs when negative thinking gains control and blocks out or distorts any positive messages. A can't-do attitude is the result.

- **Lack of trust.** A sense of cynicism can pervade a work environment if management claims one set of positive values, such as loyalty and dedication, but then acts in a way that contradicts those values, such as by retooling or downsizing.

- **Loss of collegial community.** Many people feel disconnected at work, left out, forgotten in their cubicles. This sense of isolation is a real problem for self-employed workers, but it's also a growing concern for companies that are connected through computer networks rather than community gathering spaces.

- **Job burnout.** Job burnout is a unique type of stress. It's a serious consequence of the combination of a workaholic culture and toxic stress. You may feel burned out when you feel trapped in your job, unable to see a future in it. You can't manage to handle routine tasks; you're tired, tense, and irritable; and frankly, you just don't care!

Signs of dis-stress

Some of the signs of *dis-stress*, that is, stress gone too far, are easily recognized, but many are not. If you can develop an awareness of these signs, you can judge whether you are a normal worrier or a problem worrier. Stress can affect you and your body in four areas: physical, emotional, behavioral, and mental. "Your dis-stress checklist" can help you determine whether you're suffering manifestations of dis-stress.

Levels of stress

Levels of stress can range from healthy responses in dangerous situations all the way to exaggerated and dysfunctional worry about every aspect of life. Consider your particular situation: Does the level of stress in your workplace promote energy and excitement? Are major work stressors affecting your performance or the work of those around you? Do you or your team members or direct reports show signs of toxic stress?

If stress is a problem for you or for others in your work environment, it's time to face it and deal with it. There are many ways

Your dis-stress checklist

Are you experiencing . . .	Yes	No
Pounding heart		
Elevated blood pressure		
Sweating		
Headache		
Sleep disturbances		
Skin rashes		
Trembling or tics		
Irritability and impatience		
Depression		
Fearfulness		
Low self-esteem		
Envy		
Loss of interest in your job		
Eating too much or too little		
Drinking more alcohol		
Pacing or restlessness		
Increased smoking		
Teeth grinding, nail biting, or other nervous behaviors		
Aggressive driving		
Forgetfulness		
Mind racing or going blank		
Indecisiveness		
Resistance to change		
Diminished sense of humor		
Declining productivity		

Interpreting your responses: If you answered "Yes" to more than half of these statements, you may be suffering from physical, emotional, behavioral, and mental manifestations of dis-stress.

to improve an unhealthy, stress-laden situation. The strategies for dealing with toxic stress in this guide can help most people achieve a healthier stress-performance balance. However, if you or your coworkers or direct reports get stuck, it is important to recognize the extent of the problem and get further professional help.

Taking Charge
of Stress

Acceptance—or action?

There are always parts of your life that you cannot change—who you are, where you are, and where you've been. For those facts that simply *are*, acceptance is the healthiest path to take. But for those parts of your life that you *can* change, taking charge by giving yourself the power to change is an exciting prospect. If your stress level is too high, if you worry obsessively, if you are anxious about every little thing, take a deep breath and then take charge. The following sections present basic strategies for taking charge.

Tip: Help your team or direct reports accept the unchangeable elements of the business environment and take charge of what can be changed or reformed.

Reversing the basic equation of worry

The basic equation of worry describes a negative process of increasing worry.

Increased vulnerability + decreased power = increased worry

Taking charge describes the process of reversing this basic equation: Ease worry by reducing your feeling of vulnerability and bolstering your feeling of power.

Decreased vulnerability + increased power = decreased worry

By beginning to take charge, you can decrease your sense of help-lessness, increase your power to perceive the problem more clearly and to discover positive actions you need to take to improve the situation or solve the problem, and quickly diminish the worry that was interfering with your ability to function effectively.

"If worrying can persecute us, it can also work for us, as self-preparation. No stage fright, no performance."
   —Adam Phillips

Applying the four-step approach

One way to break out of the negative stress cycle is to take this four-step approach, which gives you a structure for dealing with stress as it occurs.

- **Step 1: stop.** As soon as you begin to feel stress coming on, say, "Stop!" to yourself. For example, your computer freezes just as you're trying to finish your presentation, and you feel that rush of anxiety with failure messages flooding into your mind: "The presentation will fail; I'll fail; I'll be fired." Block those messages before they can be heard by saying, "Stop!" Repeat the message two more times: "Stop! Stop!"

- **Step 2: breathe.** The next step is to breathe. Take a deep breath, filling your diaphragm with air. Hold that breath for eight seconds, and then slowly let the air out. Just as the word "stop" blocks the negative thoughts from your mind, breathing overcomes the tendency to hold your breath when under stress. Focusing on breathing helps you to focus on your stress in a different way.

- **Step 3: reflect.** By interrupting the pattern of stress and giving yourself energy through breathing, you can now focus on the real problem, the cause of the stress. By reflecting on your stress response, you can begin to distinguish the different levels of thought and to sort out rational from irrational stress responses. You can see the practical situation more calmly and realistically and distinguish it from the distortions of your anxiety-influenced thoughts.

- **Step 4: choose.** Finally, with your attention now on the practical problem itself, you can choose to find real solutions. For example, after rebooting your computer you may discover that very little material was lost, or that even without the lost material, you'll still be able to get the information across to your audience using the old-fashioned method of talking it through. What might have seemed a disaster becomes a manageable problem that you were given the power to solve by identifying your options.

Maintaining your work/life balance

Stress occurs in most working situations, but the often conflicting demands of work and personal life can be a major source of stress, worry, and anxiety, both at work and at home. Finding a healthy balance between the two can reduce toxic stress and increase productive energy in all aspects of your life. Keep in mind the following:

- Work and personal life need to be complementary, not conflicting.

- Business priorities need to be identified and then balanced with personal concerns.

- "Whole people" are those whose skills and knowledge overlap in work and in life beyond work.

- Flexible and creative approaches to this balance enhance an employee's performance and energy for both work and personal life.

Steps for Breaking Out of the Negative Stress Cycle

1. Stop the negative messages flooding your mind.
2. Breathe by taking a deep breath and slowly letting the air out.
3. Reflect on the situation.
4. Choose to find a solution.

Turning Worry
into Action

A three-step strategy

You already have the means to change the pattern of escalating worry by using the power of your mind. The systematic *Evaluate-Plan-Remediate* approach allows you to examine the process of worry and break it down into smaller, more manageable problem units that can be solved or resolved.

For example, suppose you receive a team e-mail from your supervisor about the agenda for an upcoming budget review meeting. In the past, you've always been asked to present the target revenues for your department, but you have yet to be asked this year. You feel a twist in your stomach, a sign that worry is creeping in. Your thoughts begin to speed up: "Why haven't I been asked? Did someone else get the assignment? Did I do a poor job last time? I must be an idiot! Am I being demoted or eased out?" Using the Evaluate-Plan-Remediate worry-intervention method, you can stop the worry as soon as you start to feel it taking over.

1. **Evaluate:** "Yes, I haven't yet been asked to present the projected revenues at the budget review meeting. That's all I know right now."

2. **Plan:** "I need to get information. I should contact my supervisor and ask her directly if she expects me to present this part of the budget."

3. **Remediate:** "I'll call my supervisor and make an appointment to see her in person."

This simple sequence can replace that sense of panic with an immediate evaluation of the situation and a plan for necessary action. If you can make this process a habit every time you feel that twist in your stomach or twinge in your head, you'll turn your worry into action.

Step 1: evaluate

The key to evaluating the cause of the worry is to confront it. Don't ignore those little signals your body is giving you. They won't go away until you face what causes them. Use the following guidelines for this step.

Name the problem Just giving a name to a problem can help reduce stress because by identifying the specific problem, you've already eliminated all other possibilities. Naming makes things more manageable. Discover the stress-creating pattern that describes your situation. For example, do you take on too many responsibilities? Find it difficult to balance work and life issues? Work in the wrong job? Have problems with colleagues or supervisors? Procrastinate when a deadline looms?

Think constructively about the problem This may seem like a difficult step, but all it takes is an honest examination of your own automatic worry process. It requires that you step back and watch yourself in order to identify how your mind leaps from the bad news or perceived danger that triggers the worry to the "awfulizing" of the initial event. Apply these practices:

- **Examine your automatic thoughts.** Monitor your automatic thoughts. What words pop into your mind? Write down the words and look at them more objectively. Often you can see how exaggerated they are. For example, do you use negative descriptors (*idiot*, *stupid*) against yourself?

- **Correct errors in logic.** Next, examine your automatic thoughts for errors in logic. For example, why would your supervisor include you in the e-mail message about the budget meeting unless you had a role in that meeting? Your hasty assumption that you were being excluded is an error in logic.

- **Develop alternative hypotheses.** Even though you may leap to the worst-case scenario, there may be other hypotheses that could explain the situation. Your supervisor may have assumed that you were working on the revenue report, or she may have a different task in mind for you.

- **Revise your fundamental assumptions about yourself and your work.** Instead of calling yourself stupid and assuming that the disaster will certainly occur, start becoming your own best supporter. This may prove to be a difficult step to take because these fundamental assumptions can reflect ancient and deep-seated ways of looking at yourself and your world. However, if these assumptions are untrue and block constructive thoughts, they need to be replaced with healthier and more honest ones. The important thing is to discard the distortions that prevent you from achieving rational and productive solutions.

Tip: Do a reality check. Find out whether your worry has any basis in fact. Toxic worry can distort the real situation. Check to make sure that things are really as bad as they seem. Even when there is an actual problem, it may be easier to solve than you think.

Never worry alone Invite a friend to help as a listening partner. Sharing your worries with the right person can make you feel better by unloading the weight of worry. Just talking out loud about your concerns helps to sort them out and to clarify where your concerns may be valid and where you may be distorting the problem. The listener, at this point, needs simply to listen, rather than trying to solve your problems. Your goal here is to understand your own worry process and gain the power to find your own solutions.

Step 2: plan

Planning ahead can take time and may seem to be a burden, but the value of planning is a more than adequate return on your time investment. Planning can intercept the toxic worry and replace it with effective action. Here are some practices you can apply in advance.

Get the facts Wise worry confronts real problems. Toxic worry exaggerates and misrepresents reality. Brooding about the "what-if" possibilities passively burns up your energy. So get active! Find out what the truth of the matter is. Go to the sources of information, and don't rely on hearsay, gossip, or your own vivid imagination.

Tip: Get help from the right sources—people who have the information you need. Often you don't have the information or tools necessary to attack a problem. Instead of worrying, take control by getting the help you need. Find out who the authority is and where you should look for answers.

Structure your life Much worry results from unstructured living and thinking habits. A cluttered desk with files scattered about means wasted time finding the material you need and the risk of losing important information. In the same way, a mind cluttered with "what-if" possibilities can hide the "that-is" reality. Worried people typically spend more time and energy worrying than they do accomplishing productive tasks.

Structuring your life is being kind and considerate to your-self—organizing your desk helps *you* find things. Structuring your life reduces your risk of losing vital files, information, keys—and also prevents you from losing perspective. Use structure as an anti-anxiety agent: lists, reminders, schedules, rules, and budgets are all methods of structuring your life for your own benefit.

Take the time to structure your space. For example, organize your desk. Use colored file folders with clear labels. Put your keys in the same spot every day. And organize your computer desktop and mailbox. Also structure your *time*:

- Set goals. Decide what you want or need to accomplish in the coming week.

- Prioritize your goals. Break them down into small, manageable activities.

- Use a date book to avoid missing appointments and to stay on target.

- Be fair to yourself: make your plan for the week reasonable.

- Match important activities to the times of your high-energy peaks—the times of the day when you feel most alert and vigorous.

- Save the simple, repetitive tasks for your low-energy periods.

- Avoid getting involved in activities that don't match your goals.

- Be sure to take breaks to restore energy—stand up and stretch, take a short walk, or chat briefly with a colleague.

Step 3: remediate

The next step is to find a remedy for toxic worry. Reason, planning, and action are powerful antidotes to the paralysis of stress and worry. Consider these guidelines.

Take direct action If you've evaluated the problem and planned what you can do about it, then go ahead, take the plunge and just do it! Make the phone call, change your behavior, clean up that desk, connect with a friend, or confront that difficult colleague. Taking action is empowering. Your feeling of vulnerability and your toxic worry will fade.

Let it go Why let go? No matter how much you may want to effect a change, some problems can't be solved by any action on your part. You just have to wait and see how things turn out. Worrying about the matter won't help. For example, if your supervisor suddenly announces a major reorganization, you can't do anything about it until the event happens and you have more information about how it will affect you. You just have to sit tight and wait. Or perhaps you're up for a big promotion, but you won't find out about the decision for a month. You will be better off in every way—physically, emotionally, and mentally—if you can let the worry go until later.

What does letting go mean? Letting go means giving up your sense of control, and this can be difficult to do. Often people feel that if they worry enough, they might affect the outcome. But in those cases and times when control doesn't help and worry only hurts, it's worth the effort to give up both worry and control.

How can you let worry go? Different people have different ways. Some find that meditation helps. Some listen to music or sing a song. Try putting your worry in the palm of your hand and blowing it away. Close your eyes and imagine the worry putting on its coat and hat and walking slowly out of the room. The important thing for you is to say goodbye to useless worry.

Tip: If there's nothing you can do about a problem (or nothing more, if you already worked on it)—if it's simply out of your control—you have to let the worry go. Blow it away, and start a new project, read a different book, walk another path.

Connecting
with Others

Making connections

The Evaluate-Plan-Remediate approach uses reason, logic, and action to confront the exaggerations of toxic worry by increasing the worrier's sense of power and control. Connectedness uses the human need to connect and share with others to reduce the sense of vulnerability. Thus, both approaches help to reverse the basic equation of worry.

In the workplace, connectedness can be feeling that you are part of a company, part of a department, part of a team, working together. Connectedness can also be sharing with friends, with partners, in activities you love.

CONNECTEDNESS *n* **1:** a feeling that you are part of something larger than yourself

---

Understanding the disconnected workplace

As so many of us sit in our cubicles today, separated from our coworkers and yet not quite alone, we can feel disconnected from the people surrounding us. Entrepreneurs or home-office workers can feel even more isolated. We communicate via e-mails, voice mail, and faxes, rarely speaking one-on-one to a human voice on the telephone, much less face-to-face. With the ability to access large amounts of information on the Internet, we don't even need to speak to a librarian to get the data or knowledge we need to complete a project.

That sense of disconnectedness can aggravate our anxieties, contribute to worry, and increase stress. We can have a difficult time finding someone to talk to, someone with whom we can test our concerns in reality checks; share news, ideas, and resources; or just banter about the latest sports, politics, or company events. The obstacles to connecting that some companies create can seem daunting:

- Treating employees as robots
- Using technical communication instead of human interaction
- Encouraging a competitive desire to hoard information instead of sharing
- Separating employees physically into work cubes
- Overloading employees with extra work

Time, pressure, and competition keep employees hunched over their desks, increasing their stress and ultimately decreasing their productivity.

"Worry gives a small thing a big shadow."
    —Swedish proverb

What WOULD You Do?

Rabbit, Run

O NE MORNING, ELLEN, a manager in the customer service department, overhears a colleague talking about presenting reports at an upcoming meeting. These are reports that *Ellen* usually presents. She wonders whether she did a poor job presenting the reports last time and worries that her supervisor has asked someone else to present them this time because he wasn't satisfied with Ellen's presentation. Ellen realizes that she often feels this way—vulnerable to criticism from supervisors and peers—and she knows that this sense of vulnerability is adding to the stress she is experiencing. Whenever she finds herself wondering if she's going to be criticized, she feels like a frightened rabbit menaced by a predator. And her nervous habits, such as chewing her nails and pulling at her hair, intensify. Ellen knows she needs to address her tendency to feel vulnerable. But she's not sure precisely how to tackle the problem.

Unleashing the power of connectedness

While isolation permits toxic worry to escalate, human contact can deflate toxic worry. The human moment—when two people are face-to-face and listening to each other—gives the worrier a chance to unburden himself or herself of those anxieties, a chance to get a reality check from the listener, a chance to be reassured that he or she is not alone facing apparently overwhelming problems.

The human moment, that one-on-one connection between two people, is essential for combating negative stress and distorted worries, but other forms of positive connectedness are also important and powerful antidotes to stress and worry. Everyone in the workplace—individual employees, supervisors, and self-employed workers—needs to strive to increase their own and others' connections to people they trust and to ideas and things they care about.

Using connections to foster community

Two kinds of connectedness are vital in the workplace: connectedness to colleagues and connectedness to a mission.

Connectedness to colleagues This takes effort on your part, but it's worth it. Seek out other members of your department or team, but don't limit yourself to this group. Start by saying hello—it's as simple as that! Pause at the coffee center to chat about small things. Sit down next to a new person in the lunchroom. Ask people about their work, family, or other interests—usually people are pleased to have someone interested in them.

Individual entrepreneurs and home-office workers can make the effort to get together as a group to form a community and share their experiences—successes and problems, worries and concerns. Weekly or monthly gatherings (even Internet chat rooms) with the express purpose of connection are primarily used as professional networking tools, but they can also fulfill a human need for connectedness.

Connectedness to a mission On the job, caring about your team's projects or your company's mission can help you feel just as connected as sharing news with a colleague. Feeling as if you are a part of the whole, not just some interchangeable peg, gives you a sense of your own worth. As a supervisor, encouraging this kind of connected spirit will increase your team's productivity. As an employee, caring can help turn negative worry into positive energy.

Together, these two kinds of connectedness can produce a sense of community in the workplace that is essential for the well-being and productivity of all of its members.

Achieving quick-fix connections

Long-term positive and trusting relationships may be the best kind of anti-worry connection, but there are times when a person simply needs a quick fix. Quick-fix connections don't solve deeper problems, but they can be very useful for those occasional crises that almost everyone experiences. Reassurance and venting are two tools for achieving quick-fix connections.

Reassurance as a bandage If, for example, two different supervisors ask one employee for two separate reports due on the same day, the employee may feel panicked, overwhelmed by the enormity of the required tasks. The work may seem impossible, and anticipating failure can set off waves of toxic stress. What to do? In this situation, the employee could use some reassurance just to help make it through this tough time.

Reassurance is a type of connectedness that says to the worrier that everything will be fine. It's a kind of comfort that can soothe

the anxious mind with a counteracting voice and offer just enough encouragement to help the worrier get through the difficult time. It's easy to give and warmly received.

- **Getting reassurance.** When you need reassurance, ask for it. That's difficult for some people, but it's worth learning how to do it. Don't make someone guess from your body language or roundabout questions that you need reassurance. Just say, "Tell me everything is going to be okay." But even more important, ask the right person. Some people simply can't respond—they may be too distant or too honest. Make sure the person you ask knows when to be reassuring and when to provide his or her honest opinion.

- **Giving reassurance.** Even though it's easy to give reassurance, it may seem hard. If you've never received it yourself, if you believe a person needs to be "strong" enough to make it through without reassurance, or if you believe you always need to be honest about the prospects of success or failure, you may resist giving reassurance. However, you may be pleasantly surprised at how a little reassurance can go a long way toward turning an anxious person into a more productive one. Say the words, "It'll be fine." Give a pat on the back, a little hug, a bit of hope to build some confidence.

The problem with reassurance is that it is just a bandage used to cover a hurt. If it's the only tool used to counteract worry, it's not enough. Chronic worriers need much more than just reassurance; chronic worriers need to challenge themselves in more systematic and holistic ways.

Venting as relief Another kind of quick-fix connection is venting. If, for example, you have a bad week when everything seems to go wrong—your car breaks down, your assistant quits, your computer gets a virus, your budget request is denied—you can feel overwhelmed and begin to wonder what new catastrophe awaits. The stress of dealing with these real problems can suddenly escalate and interfere with a rational approach to problem solving. That's when not only reassurance but also a healthy session of venting can help.

Venting can offer relief by allowing you to unburden your problems. Just listing them out loud can diminish their power to assault your worried mind. Venting can be good for you! But be sure to vent to the right person. You need someone who will listen and sympathize, not someone who will brush aside your list as unimportant, and not someone who wants to solve everything for you. The purpose of venting is to ease your mind, giving you the mental space to return to the problems with renewed energy to deal with them as needed.

What You COULD Do.

Remember Ellen and her desire to feel less vulnerable?

Here's what the mentor suggests:

Ellen is correct in seeing feelings of vulnerability for what they are: a major part of the worry equation (vulnerability + powerlessness = worry). She could reduce her feelings of vulnerability through two means. First, she could connect with colleagues, perhaps by systematically scheduling lunches and other social interactions with members of her department and people from other departments. Connecting with others is actually a powerful antidote to stress and worry because it eases feelings of isolation and therefore vulnerability. By interacting with others, Ellen can also conduct reality checks on her concerns, as well as share news, ideas, and resources. She may discover she's not alone in her struggle to manage stress.

Ellen could also remind herself that she has consistently done a good job and that her supervisor has given her positive performance reviews. When people are stressed, they tend to engage in negative self-talk—such as overgeneralizing or blaming themselves inappropriately for problems. By replacing such thought patterns with more positive self-talk, Ellen can reframe the way

continued

she perceives stressful events and reduce her feelings of vulnerability. For example, if she were to ask her supervisor if he expects her to present the usual reports at the next meeting, she may learn that he does—and that her colleague was actually talking about a possible new *format* for the printed reports.

Connecting
with Yourself

Using self-talk

Connecting with yourself may be one of the most effective strategies for challenging stress and winning. As we grow up and learn about the world around us, we develop automatic thoughts to help us sort through our perceptions and experiences. If these automatic thoughts are healthy and constructive, we cope with our life in positive ways. However, chronic worriers often subject themselves to negative automatic thoughts that contribute to their worry and stress.

Eroding the destructive power of negative thoughts

Negative self-talk, what you say to yourself, contributes directly to your stress. Self-talk is related to your internal assumptions and beliefs, and it is typically automatic, familiar, and unconscious. For example, our bodies can't sort out the experiences we have from the events we imagine. As we imagine a bad outcome—say, being fired from a job—our bodies react to the thought as though it were actually happening. All the physical reactions that would occur in a dangerous situation will occur in an imagined one, too.

Also, we talk to ourselves constantly, and if those messages are negative and critical ("How could I do such a foolish thing!") or name-calling ("I'm an idiot!")—we start to believe them. Finally, we rarely stop to consider what we are saying to ourselves. We don't counter the criticisms, for example, with understanding or forgiveness. In other words, we don't test our own assumptions. Because we don't counter negative thoughts—such as, "I know I won't get that raise"—those thoughts can become self-fulfilling.

Tuning in to your self-talk

To accurately tune into your negative self-talk, you must first identify your automatic thoughts. These are spontaneous thoughts that may or may not reflect the reality of your situation.

To begin, think about what you tell yourself when you first arrive at the office in the morning. Is the message positive or negative? Is there a familiar feel to the message? For example, do you see your desk and think, "I'll never get everything done today"? If so, is this message accurate? Could you be distorting or exaggerating the situation?

Identifying and avoiding common mind traps

Automatic thoughts often fall into categories called *mind traps.* These mind traps are irrational beliefs that can lead you astray from a clear and realistic perception of your world. Identifying the ones you use and are comfortable with will help you challenge them. Consider how your automatic thinking might fall into the traps listed in the table, "About mind traps."

About mind traps

Mind traps	What they are
"Should" statements	"I should do this. I must do that." You motivate yourself with "shoulds" and then feel guilty.
All-or-nothing thinking	"One mistake, and total failure will result." You see things in extremes of black or white, all bad or all good.
Overgeneralizations	"This always happens." You set a pattern of inevitability to an event that happens once or twice.
Mental filtering	"This one mistake ruins everything." You see only the negative side to an event and ignore the positive one.
Rejection of positive experiences	"The team complimented my work just to be polite." You accept only the negative messages.
Jumping to conclusions	"Our department is being restructured. I know I'll be fired." Without bothering to get the facts, you assume the worst.
Emotional reasoning	"I feel like a loser, so I must be a loser." You assume your negative feelings represent reality.
Labeling	"I'm so stupid and irresponsible to be late for that meeting!" You label yourself negatively.
Personalizing	"The proposal was rejected because I was on the team." You assign cause and blame to yourself inappropriately.

Challenging self-talk distortions

Once you can identify the mind traps that you easily fall into, begin to challenge them, one by one. The table, "Mind-trap remedies" offers possible remedies for common mind traps.

Mind-trap remedies

Mind traps	Remedies
"Should" statements	Use the verb "want" instead of "should." Give yourself some flexibility in deciding what you want to do.
All-or-nothing thinking	Don't make black-or-white judgments. Think of the in-between points or percentages (for example, 40% or 75%).
Overgeneralizations	Examine the evidence. Is something always true? Or has it happened two times out of the past five?
Mental filtering	Look for the positive side as well as the negative. Focus on solving the problem.
Rejection of positive experiences	Acknowledge and accept the reality of positive experiences or events.
Jumping to conclusions	Get the facts first. See if the evidence supports your conclusion.
Emotional reasoning	Step away from just your emotions, and try to look at yourself as others see you.
Labeling	Describe the behavior, not yourself. If you make a mistake, acknowledge the mistake; don't blame yourself.
Personalizing	Make yourself prove that you are responsible for the situation. What is the evidence?

Choosing positive self-talk

Choosing positive self-talk over existing mind traps isn't easy. However, adopting a positive outlook is critical to avoiding workplace stress. To reprogram your self-talk, start slowly. Consider how you can reframe the way you perceive events. Reframing is a way of restating negative self-talk into positive affirmation. It puts the picture or experience into a different frame, so that you can look at it in a new way. Consider the worst-case scenario of a given situation. For example, what if you do get fired after a merger? What would happen to you? What new opportunities might emerge from that event? In other words, look at a situation from as many different views as possible. What can you learn about it? A situation that might seem disastrous could offer exciting new opportunities. What seems like a terrible mistake may be a great chance to learn.

Also think about how you can affirm yourself. Give yourself reassurance and support. Positive and constructive self-talking takes practice; at first, it may seem uncomfortable. But keep on doing it. Tell yourself that you're fine, that you'll make it, and that you deserve that raise. Give yourself credit when it's due. The positive alternatives will gain strength because they actually make more sense.

REFRAMING *v* **1:** restating destructive self-talk into positive ways of perceiving events

---

Letting Your Body Help You Relieve Stress

Understanding stress's impact on the body

There are times when no matter how much you evaluate, plan, and remediate, no matter how connected you become to others and to your own feelings, you may still be burdened by those real situations that deserve your attention and concern. Or you may still feel those waves of anxiety and stress in spite of how thoughtful, analytical, or connected you may be. One important way to manage your stress, whatever its source, is to exercise your body. Changing your physical state can help change your mental state.

After all, stress has a direct impact on your body. In the short term, it gives you that energy surge and alertness you need to confront a threatening situation. However, prolonged stress puts an unhealthy strain on your body. Prolonged stress can:

- Raise your cholesterol level

- Cause your arteries to restrict, limiting blood flow to the heart

- Disrupt your digestive process and result in stomach acid, constipation, diarrhea, ulcers, or even cancer of the bowels

- Stimulate migraine headaches, asthma attacks, or other allergic reactions

Committing to exercise

The easiest, cheapest, and most natural antidote to worry is exercise. Exercise benefits your brain by:

- Reducing tension

- Easing aggression and frustration

- Providing an increased sense of well-being

- Improving sleep

- Aiding concentration

Exercise is also good for almost every other part of your body—heart, circulation, bones, respiratory system, skin, and so on. And it helps you reduce your weight, lower your blood pressure, and regulate your blood sugar.

Worry tends to put your body in a frozen, unmoving state. Exercise helps you break out of the immobility. So start by simply moving. Rock and sway. Get up and stretch. Even better, take a walk or climb some stairs. Even those brief physical efforts can help clear your mind of the weight of worry.

Better yet, get in the habit of exercising on a regular basis—three to four times a week, if possible. Choose something you enjoy doing—walking, running, bicycling, inline skating, hiking, swimming, rowing, playing tennis or basketball. If you don't enjoy it, you won't keep it up.

Eating healthfully

Eating is another way to cope with stress. If you consume junk food as a response to a stressful day, food has become a negative coping response for you. But if you eat a healthy and varied diet, your body will be better able to deal with the normal or higher levels of stress you face each day.

Some ways to achieve healthy eating habits include those listed here.

- **Maintain a healthy weight.** Toxic stress can affect your weight by causing you to under- or overeat. Either way, your body won't have the optimum level of energy it needs to function effectively. First, determine the healthiest body weight for you, taking into account that this number varies by height, gender, and age. Then, if you do need to adjust your body weight, choose a slow, steady weight-loss or -gain diet.

- **Eat a variety of food.** Not only is it more interesting to vary your diet, but you also give your body the full range of nutrients it needs. Eating plenty of vegetables, fruit, and grains is especially healthy.

- **Reduce the level of fat and cholesterol in your diet.** Eat foods that are broiled, baked, or steamed rather than fried. Limit your intake of animal products such as egg yolks.

- **Moderate your consumption of alcohol and caffeine.** Alcohol is a depressant and can disturb your sleep, which only worsens stress. Caffeine is a stimulant and can amplify feelings of nervousness.

Sleeping restfully

Insomnia can be caused by stress, and lack of sleep can aggravate the level of stress. This can cause you to become more tense, irritable, and anxious. People vary in the amount of sleep they need, but your body will tell you what's right for you. Pay attention to how you feel in the morning after more or less sleep. Then make an effort to get the amount of sleep that's right for you. If you are having problems sleeping, try some of these simple sleep-improving activities.

- **Reduce your intake of caffeinated beverages and alcohol.** These substances tend to disrupt your sleep.

- **Exercise regularly.** You'll burn off tension from the day and more easily clear your mind before going to bed.

- **Plan the next day's activities early in the evening.** You'll give yourself time to clear your head before going to bed.

- **Make your sleeping environment as quiet and dark as possible.** Quiet and darkness are especially conducive to sound sleep.

- **Establish a routine for going to sleep.** For example, if you get into the habit of having a warm glass of milk or reading for half an hour before drifting off to sleep, these behaviors will eventually serve as strong signals that it's time to sleep.

- **Use relaxation techniques to help yourself fall asleep.** For example, some people find it helpful to count backward from 25, 50, or 100. Others imagine each set of muscles melting like butter.

- **If you can't sleep, get out of bed and do something soothing until you feel sleepy again.** Lying in bed and trying your hardest to fall asleep will only lead to frustration.

"There is more to life than just increasing its speed."
—Mahatma Gandhi

Mastering the relaxation response

The relaxation response is a structured approach to using breathing and relaxation to counter the negative effects of stress. It is a deliberate and controlled technique that is opposite to the body's natural fight-or-flight stress response in the face of apparent danger or a perceived threatening situation. While the body's fight-or-flight mode causes an increase in the heart rate and breathing, the relaxation response reverses these bodily states.

When you find yourself feeling unnecessary stress, apply this simple technique to counteract the negative effects of stress on your body. To prepare, you will need:

- **A quiet environment.** Find a quiet, calm place; a private room; or a space with no distractions.

- **A mental device.** Choose a constant stimulus of a single-syllable sound or word, such as the word *one*. Repeat that sound silently or softly over and over again. Focus solely on that sound.

- **A passive attitude.** Disregard all distracting thoughts. Simply let yourself be completely passive.

- **A comfortable position.** Sit in a comfortable chair, preferably with neck and head support. Loosen all tight-fitting clothes. Prop your feet up, if possible.

To induce the relaxation response, follow these steps.

1. Sit in a comfortable position.

2. Close your eyes.

3. Deeply relax your muscles, starting with your toes and moving up to your face and head.

4. Breathe through your nose. As you breathe out, say the sound or word you have chosen silently or softly to yourself. Breathe in. Breathe out and say the word again. Breathe in.

5. Keep repeating the breathing pattern and the sound for 20 minutes. Open your eyes to check the time, but do not use an alarm or other sharp noise.

6. When you finish, sit quietly for several minutes, at first with your eyes closed and then with your eyes open.

After using this technique, most people feel calm and relaxed, but perhaps the most important benefit is an immediate lowering of blood pressure. And the interruption of stressful and worried thoughts can enable you to focus more clearly on the real situation.

Tip: Relax whenever and wherever you can. Practice relaxation techniques whenever you start to feel the first signs of tension, worry, or stress. While quick exercises that you can do almost anywhere are helpful, find the time and space for longer, more meditative relaxation—these exercises are more beneficial in the long run.

Practicing Good Stress Habits

Avoiding stress stimulants

Stress stimulants surround us in our busy, modern world. Try to avoid those superficial stress arousers and focus on only those matters that are truly important. For example, *shun negative office politics and workplace conflicts.* Intra- and interdepartmental rivalries can create an artificial sense of competition and crisis. Genuine teamwork and shared activities create a more effective and productive environment. If you have the power to move your colleagues away from conflict and toward a connected community, you will be helping not only yourself but the organization as well.

Also *limit excessive media stimulants.* Too much Internet time can aggravate tension due to the flashing advertisements, overly busy pages, frustratingly slow downloads, and startling pop-up menus. Skip exaggerated disaster news stories; one of their purposes is to arouse your level of worry. Avoid watching too much television—it's another source of extraneous information and pressure.

Finally, *restrict your intake of caffeinated beverages, alcohol, and sugar.* They may seem to help give you what you want at the moment—whether it's being alert with caffeine, or gaining a quick energy pick-me-up with sugar, or relaxing with an alcoholic drink—but these effects are all superficial. Overuse can produce the opposite effect.

Adopting stress busters

Incorporate stress busters into your everyday routine to help you deal with those moments when your body tenses up at the thought of another long budget meeting, at the message you received from your supervisor to see him immediately, or at the workaholic's announcement that she worked all weekend. Stress busters can become easy and natural ways to help you endure those anxious moments and enjoy your life and work.

Try "minis"   Minis are shorter versions of the relaxation response technique that you can use quickly whenever you feel tension beginning to grip you. Taking the following actions will help to reduce stress if you don't have a lot of time.

- Take a deep breath and hold it for several seconds. Then let your breath out very slowly while repeating your focus word.

- Put your right hand just under your navel. Focus on breathing down to your navel. As you breathe in the first time, say the number *ten*. Breathe out. Then breathe in and say the number *nine*. Breathe out. Continue until you reach *zero*.

- Breathe in through your nose and breathe out through your mouth ten times. Notice how cool the air feels when you inhale and how warm it is when you exhale.

- Imagine air as a cloud. As you breathe, envision that the air comes to you as a cloud, filling you and then leaving you.

Enjoy humor Laughing can transform that rigidly tight facial expression of tension into more relaxed and flexible features. Humor is also a way to reframe negative self-talk into something more positive and fun.

Step back from the worry and strain of the job, and look for the funny side of things.

- Find the humor in everyday situations. Watch out for coincidences, ironies, and contradictions.

- Think about playing at your work. Many routine tasks can be seen as game-playing moves.

- Collect cartoons to decorate your workspace.

- Exaggerate something to the point of absurdity. Step out of your usual bounds, or say the unexpected occasionally.

- Take your standard negative self-talk lines, and rephrase them into funny talk. For example, change "This always happens to me" to "And I only volunteer 60% of the time!"

NOTE: Don't mistake humor for ridicule. Laughing at someone or at the expense of someone is not nearly as funny as it is hurtful. Real humor is based on respect and includes everyone in the fun.

Take a break Our bodies and minds need time-outs, breaks from our work and activities. Pay attention to your stress and energy levels. When you feel tension rising and energy falling, take a break. Some stress-reducing changes in your work pattern include:

- Listening to music

- Going for a walk

- Chatting with friends

- Climbing some stairs

These are brief, daily breaks. Be sure to schedule longer breaks such as extended weekends or short getaways as well. Ride out into the country, stay in a bed-and-breakfast, go hiking or fishing, or simply read a good book. A complete and longer change of pace can help you perceive your work world in a whole new way—with less worry and more energy.

All of these activities can reduce stress and restore energy. Moments of leisure, relaxation, and pleasure mean less worry and dis-stress.

Tips and Tools

Tools for
Managing Stress

Life Changes as Stressors Checklist

Change, even positive change, involves stress. Listed below are some common stressful events. Check off the ones that apply to you, and add them up to get a picture of your current stress level and some of its sources. Use this information to select strategies that can help you manage or diminish your stress level.

Personal Changes

- ☐ Personal injury/illness/handicap
- ☐ Pregnancy (your or partner's)
- ☐ End of a relationship
- ☐ Life changes (such as a certain birthday, menopause)
- ☐ Change in self-worth

- ☐ Change in financial status
- ☐ Sexual concerns or difficulties
- ☐ Decision to quit smoking or other substance use
- ☐ Decision to diet
- ☐ Values conflict

Other:

Family Changes

- ☐ Marriage
- ☐ Family member(s) leaving home
- ☐ New family member(s)
- ☐ Separation/divorce
- ☐ Trouble with in-laws or other family members

- ☐ Partner starting or stopping a job
- ☐ Illness/healing of a family member
- ☐ Death of a close friend or family member
- ☐ Parent/child tensions

Other:

Work Changes

- ☐ Change in workload
- ☐ Change in pay
- ☐ Start of a new job
- ☐ Promotion/demotion
- ☐ Change in relationships at work

- ☐ New supervisor
- ☐ Retirement
- ☐ Change in hours
- ☐ Change in job security/layoff
- ☐ Merger or acquisition

Other:

Environmental Changes

- ☐ Natural disaster (earthquake, fire, flood)
- ☐ War or conflict
- ☐ Move to a new house or apartment
- ☐ Move to a new neighborhood

- ☐ Move to a new city
- ☐ Move to a new climate
- ☐ Move to a new culture or country
- ☐ Remodeling project
- ☐ Crime in neighborhood

Other:

Workplace Stress Assessment

*Use this informal assessment to help identify (either by yourself or with a work group)
the current level of positive and negative stress in your work environment.
Then discuss or brainstorm strategies that can either increase the positive energy
level or diminish the unhealthy dis-stress.*

Positive Stress

I think the current level of **positive, energizing** stress in my (our) workplace is: (Check one.)

☐ low ☐ moderately low ☐ average ☐ moderately high ☐ high

Positive sources of energizing stress include: (Check all that apply.)

☐ Challenging but attainable goals
☐ The ability and resources to meet critical deadlines
☐ Team spirit, a "we-can-do-it" attitude
☐ Diverse or innovative assignments that stretch employees

☐ Effective leadership that motivates
☐ Solution of new problems
☐ The opportunity to learn new skills
☐ The resources to deal effectively with a crisis

Others:

Ideas I have to increase energizing stress (for example, a friendly competition) are:

Negative Stress

I think the current level of **negative, toxic** stress in my (our) workplace is: (Check one.)

☐ low ☐ moderately low ☐ average ☐ moderately high ☐ high

Negative stress is being shown in: (Check all that apply.)

☐ Increased irritability or temper outbursts
☐ Conflicts between team members
☐ Increased absenteeism or numbers of sick days
☐ Higher levels of errors and mistakes

☐ Overall reduction in productivity
☐ Increase in employee burnout, turnover
☐ People "tuning out," decreased engagement

Others:

Ideas I have to reduce toxic stress are:

The single action that, if implemented, would make the greatest positive difference is:

---

continued

Workload

How would you rate your workload (or that of the group)?

☐ Too low   ☐ Just right   ☐ Too high

Is this situation temporary, long-standing, or subject to change?

Is the workload stimulating or overwhelming?

If the workload needs adjustment, are there any work processes (how the work is done) that could be changed, eliminated, or modified? Which ones?

Are there opportunities to change the amount of work by adjusting deadlines, outsourcing, hiring more temporary or permanent help, or taking other measures? Can you rotate assignments? Take some time off? Other ideas to prevent overload or burnout?

Test Yourself

This section offers ten multiple-choice questions to help you identify your baseline knowledge of the essentials of managing stress. Answers to the questions are given at the end of the test.

1. All stress and worry should be avoided. True or false?

    a. True.

    b. False.

2. Some of the most common sources of stress in the workplace are:

    a. Physical illnesses.

    b. Changes in the workplace and an unhealthy work environment.

    c. Concerns about home life's effect on work.

3. The four steps for breaking out of the negative stress cycle are:

    a. Breathe. Reflect. Choose. Act.

    b. Consult friends. Relax. Get a massage. Take a walk.

    c. Stop. Breathe. Reflect. Choose.

4. In what ways can connectedness help reduce stress?

    a. Connecting with solutions can reduce stressful situations.

    b. Connections with trusted people, particularly colleagues, can provide you with reassurance and can help you gain perspective and perhaps new ideas for solutions.

    c. Offices that are technologically connected help reduce the stress of dealing with outdated networks or a lack of networks.

5. Chronic worriers often subject themselves to negative automatic thoughts that contribute to their worry and stress. True or false?

    a. True.

    b. False.

6. Which of the following is the easiest, cheapest, and most natural antidote to worry?

    a. Exercising.

    b. Eating healthfully.

    c. Sleeping restfully.

7. What do you need to prepare for the relaxation response?

    a. A dark room, a bed or cot, and soft music.

    b. A spiritual guide.

    c. A quiet environment, a mental device, a passive attitude, and a comfortable position.

8. Which of the following activities can be used as stress busters?

   a. Playing video games.

   b. Laughing about an amusing story.

   c. Taking a coffee break.

9. Which of the following is *not* an effective response to a colleague who tells you he's extremely worried about something?

   a. Use body language to show your concern.

   b. Suggest several possible solutions to his problem.

   c. Provide occasional verbal acknowledgment.

10. The most effective way to counter the negative effects of toxic worry is to:

   a. Reverse the worry equation by increasing your sense of power and decreasing your sense of vulnerability.

   b. Solve the problems that are causing the worry.

   c. Ensure that you get sufficiently restful sleep.

Answers to test questions

1, b. This statement is actually false. All stress and worry should *not* be avoided. Some stress is actually good because it can provide you with the extra energy you need to deal with situations. To the extent that stress helps you prepare for difficult times, you can benefit from it.

2, b. One common source of stress in the workplace is change in the workplace—whether a positive change (such as a new assignment) or a negative one (such as an increase in workload). Another major source of stress is an unhealthy work environment marked by interpersonal conflicts or confusing expectations.

3, c. These four steps are effective in breaking the negative stress cycle. When you stop, you block the negative messages you're telling yourself. When you breathe, you calm your body. Then you can reflect on the problem and choose the best action to take.

4, b. Connections with trusted people are the most powerful antidote to stress because those individuals can listen to you and help you see a stressful situation in a different light. Remember one of the first rules in taking charge of worry and stress: Never worry alone!

5, a. Chronic worriers tend to make their problems worse by listening to their own negative automatic thoughts instead of looking at the actual situation. To combat chronic worrying, you can reshape such negative self-talk into more positive and healthy messages.

6, a. Exercise helps you break out of the physical immobility that stress often causes. Even brief physical efforts, such as standing up and stretching, can clear your mind of the weight of worry. Exercise reduces tension, eases aggression and frustration, increases your sense of well-being, improves sleep, and aids concentration.

7, c. You don't need much to prepare for the relaxation response. All you really need is a quiet environment where you can focus on relaxing. Then you find a comfortable position, concentrate on a single word or sound, and push away distracting thoughts.

8, b. Humor is a wonderful antidote to stress, and laughter is a natural and healthy way to release tension and put aside serious thoughts for awhile. Try finding the humor in your everyday life—but remember not to confuse genuine humor with ridicule. Humor enriches us all; ridicule hurts us all.

9, b. To listen effectively to a worried colleague, it's best not to try to solve the problem but instead to understand it. If you want to comment, do so only on what your colleague is describing, rather than offering possible solutions to the problem. In addition, use body language to show your concern and provide occasional verbal acknowledgment, such as "I understand" or "I see."

10, a. In any stressful situation, you can reduce the negative effects of toxic worry by increasing your sense of power and control and decreasing your sense of vulnerability. Strategies for increasing power and decreasing vulnerability include structuring your activities, connecting with people who can listen, and taking care of your health. All of these strategies give you the power to better manage your stress.

Frequently Asked Questions

How common are stress-related problems at work?

Extremely common. With heavy workloads, career pressure, and demands for increased productivity in almost all areas of the workplace, stress is a constant factor in our professional lives. Some stress is good—it gets people going—but too much can have the opposite effect. Excessive stress is repetitive and frustrating with no reward and no satisfaction, and it can become toxic, doing real damage to your mind and body.

Don't I have to be stressed to succeed in today's professional environment?

To a degree, yes. Stress does stimulate performance. Some people thrive in a demanding, high-stress world. They are energized by the fast-paced working style, the demands of multitasking, and the excitement of stiff competition. But most managers can't keep up that pace for long without physical and emotional consequences. The most successful managers tend to be those who prioritize their tasks, delegate responsibilities, and know when to leave their work problems behind them.

How can I tell whether my worry is productive or toxic?

It's important to tell the difference between positive stress and toxic worry. If you feel good about what you're doing, if you're producing excellent work on time and under budget, then enjoy yourself! But if you're worried and anxious, unable to concentrate on your work, or unhappy about even going to work, then the stress you feel is poisoning your life—at work and at home.

What are some of the signs of toxic stress?

Some signs of toxic stress are subtle and difficult to detect, while others are clearly recognizable. The most common indicators are changes in behavior such as decreased productivity, creativity, motivation, or confidence; increased irritability, fatigue, or pessimism; increased use of alcohol or other drugs; and increased physical ailments with no apparent cause. In practical terms, you may be dealing with a toxic level of stress if you find yourself canceling appointments, failing in an interview, or refusing to fly on an airplane just because you're too anxious.

Why is it important to talk with someone about the problem?

One of the first rules for managing stress is *never worry alone.* Talk with someone you trust. Why? Talking helps you feel more in control because it lets you know you're not alone—you're sharing the burden with another person. Your talking partner can ease your mind by reassuring you that you're okay or that the problem can be solved. He or she may also help you reflect on the situation and get the facts straight. When you're stressed, you tend to exaggerate the situation, making it worse in your mind. A talking partner can offer a different point of view—a different way of seeing the situation.

How do deep-breathing exercises help manage stressful moments?

Deep breathing can help in several ways. First, the very act of taking a deep breath helps you relax—it slows the heart rate and the respiratory rate, and it keeps the pH level of the blood stable. Just *noticing* your breathing takes your mind off the problem and puts it onto your body. Also, many people tend to hold their breath when stressed—deep breathing forces them to get oxygen back into their systems.

To Learn More

Notes and articles

Cohen, Sacha. "De-Stress for Success." *Training & Development* (November 1997).

This article provides practical ideas for reducing stress in the workplace, for example, how to improve the quality of your work environment, how to control information overload, and how to give your body a break.

Gary, Loren. "Fighting the Enemy Within." *Harvard Management Update* (February 2002).

In the uncertainty and gloom of a recession, employees naturally worry that they'll be included in the next round of layoffs. And, anxious to secure the necessary financial and human resources for their key projects, managers have to fight to keep their units intact. In such an environment, it's no wonder that negative office politics are intensified. Although you can't expect to root politics out completely, the advice given in this article is intended to help you head off the game playing instead of teaching you how to play.

Harvard Business School Publishing. "How to Get People on Board." *Harvard Management Update* (June 2000).

This article takes a leader's point of view in helping employees cope with change, shows managers how to identify sources of anxiety, and describes what managers can do to facilitate the process of change.

Laabs, Jennifer. "Overload: What's Causing It, and How to Solve It." *Workforce* (January 1999).

In this useful article, Laabs gives managers ideas for helping their direct reports avoid or manage work overload. She also points out that in order to help your team become more productive, you must first understand the cause of excess work and then work to resolve the situation.

Books

Benson, Herbert. *The Relaxation Response.* New York: Avon Books, 2000.

In an updated and expanded version of this best-selling classic, Benson describes the physiological basis of the relaxation response and its benefits in counteracting the negative effects of stress; he then takes readers through detailed steps to achieve this state of relaxation.

Breier, Mark. *The 10-Second Internet Manager.* New York: Random House, 2000.

As suggested by the title, this book provides many practical, quick tips for coping with the Internet age. For example, his advice on dealing with e-mail—often overwhelming in today's workplace—is right to the point: "Delete, divert, delay, or deal with it," but make the decision immediately.

Hallowell, Edward M. *Connect*. New York: Pantheon Books, 1999.

The most recent book by this topic's expert, *Connect* describes twelve important ways we can make connections with our families, friends, colleagues, activities, ideas, and ourselves! A tremendously important guide for dealing with the human issues of loneliness and alienation—both in the workplace and beyond.

Hallowell, Edward M. *Worry*. New York: Ballantine Books, 1997.

The title of this book says it all—here Dr. Hallowell takes a wide and deep look at worry and offers tips, guides, and programs for dealing with the toxic worry so many of us struggle with in today's hectic and stressful world.

Other learning source

www.drhallowell.com

Go to this Web site to find out more about this topic's subject matter expert, Dr. Edward Hallowell, his newsletter, and the Hallowell Center.

Sources for Managing Stress

We would like to acknowledge the sources who aided in developing this topic.

Benson, Herbert. *The Relaxation Response*. New York: Avon Books, 2000.

———. "Your Innate Asset for Combating Stress." *Harvard Business Review* (July-August 1974).

———, and Eileen M. Stuart. *The Wellness Book: The Comprehensive Guide to Maintaining Health and Treating Stress-Related Illness*. New York: Simon & Schuster, 1993.

Berman, Mark L. "Avoiding Burnout through Personal Energy Management." *American Society for Training and Development* (February 1995).

Cohen, Sacha. "De-Stress for Success." *Training & Development* (November 1997).

Davidson, Jeff. "Avoiding Job Burnout," an online program at www.youachieve.com.

Friedman, Stewart D., Perry Christensen, and Jessica DeGroot. "Work and Life: The End of the Zero-Sum Game." *Harvard Business Review* (November-December 1998).

Hallowell, Edward M. Personal conversations with author, October 2000.

———. *Connect*. New York: Pantheon Books, 1999.

———. *Worry*. New York: Ballantine Books, 1997.

Harvard Management Update editors. "How to Get People on Board." *Harvard Management Update* (June 2000).

Laabs, Jennifer. "Overload: What's Causing It, and How to Solve It." *Workforce* (January 1999).

Rosenthal, David S., and Kenneth L. Minaker. *Stress Management Guidebook*. Harvard University Health Services Good Health Management Series. Cambridge, MA: Harvard University Health Services, 1996.

Notes

Notes

Notes

Notes

Notes

Notes